AF578254

Unveiled: Voices Rising in Verse

Poems Inspired by Shakespeare's Heroines and Their Unspoken Emotions

By

Simar Walia

Dedication

For my mom and dad, who got me here.

Preface

This collection of poems represents a journey of creative exploration and personal growth that began in grade 9, when I had the opportunity to write my first dramatic monologue. Tasked with crafting a poem in this form, I chose to delve into *The Merchant of Venice* and give voice to the character of Portia. This process of researching the play, analyzing literary devices, and crafting my own poem ignited a passion for poetry that I wanted to nurture and expand upon. What began as an academic assignment soon became a path of artistic discovery.

As I continued to explore different poetic forms—ranging from ballads and sestinas to sonnets and laments—I sought to deepen my understanding of these techniques. I wanted to master various forms of expression, using poetry as a way to channel the emotions and complexities of the characters that have long fascinated me. Giving voice to Shakespeare's heroines, many of whom are often silenced or overshadowed by the actions of others, became a personal goal. Through these poems, I sought to amplify their inner worlds, allowing their stories to be told in their own words.

This collection is both a reflection of the technical skills I have developed and a manifestation of my personal connection to the characters whose voices I've sought to explore. Each poem has been crafted with attention to form, device, and structure, as I sought to learn and refine my craft. The creative process behind these poems has been one of both discovery and self-expression, allowing me to delve into the heart of these powerful women from Shakespeare's works, and ultimately, to enhance my understanding of poetry as a whole.

In creating these poems, I not only embraced my passion for poetic form but also learned to give depth and complexity to the voices of the women whose stories have long resonated with me. I hope that through these poems, the heroines of Shakespeare's plays are brought to life in a way that feels both personal and authentic, offering new insights into their characters while celebrating the beauty and versatility of poetic form. This collection is more than just a reinterpretation of Shakespeare's work; it's a way of reimagining the role of women in literature. By giving these heroines their own space to speak, I hope to challenge conventional narratives and provoke thought about the ways in which women's stories have been told—and untold—throughout history.

I hope that as you read these poems, you'll see these women as I do—not as secondary figures, but as complex, powerful beings with stories worth telling.

Index

Desdemona** from **Othello

Ballad

This poem is a ballad, a narrative form of poetry with roots in the oral traditions of medieval Europe. Characterized by its rhythmic and melodic structure, a ballad typically features short stanzas with a consistent rhyme scheme, telling a story of love, loss, or adventure. The repetition of lines and refrains enhances its emotional resonance, while the simple yet powerful language draws the reader into the unfolding drama, giving the poem a timeless, lyrical quality.

Overview

The ballad form, with its rhythmic cadence and emotive storytelling, is the ideal medium for Desdemona to expose her raw vulnerability. It reflects the rise and fall of her passion and heartbreak, mirroring the ebb and flow of her tumultuous journey. Through this lyrical structure, Desdemona's suppressed emotions come to life, offering a poignant glimpse into her enduring love and the resilience of her spirit, even in the face of betrayal.

The Last Betrayal

They disdained, they discriminated, they defied,
When thee hand claimed mine as bride.
Your age, your skin, a forbidden ache,
Yet yours and mine love collides.

Your hypnotic smile,
Evocative chronicles unceasing, your best virtue, piercing my heart,
Laughing beneath venetian skies,
Who doth know I'd be so enchanted and lost?

Yet darkness moved, crows cawed,
My betrayal, you say, stung like a snake?
Your vindictive words, cut through my veins,
The handkerchief which ached and tears which flowed for Cassio.
I can see the unseen future, a chilling shroud,
My life departing fading into the starry nights,
Spreading the wedding sheets,
Trying to feel every last inch of our love,
To dissolve your betrayal into undying trust,
A fading spark replacing fear with luck.

Forgiving you, with my last breath,
For even, fractured love subdues death.

Ophelia from **Hamlet**

Lament

This poem is a lament, a poetic form that conveys profound grief, sorrow, or mourning, often in an intensely emotional and raw voice. Laments are typically unstructured or loosely structured, allowing the speaker's anguish to flow freely and authentically. They often use vivid imagery and evocative language to articulate deep internal struggles, unfiltered emotions, and a longing for solace or resolution amidst despair.

Overview

This lament captures Ophelia's suppressed grief and anguish, offering a raw, unfiltered voice to her internal struggles and despair. The vivid imagery reflects on a life shaped by control and others' expectations, confronting her identity as a mere instrument. The poem culminates in her desperate cry for autonomy and a final act of self determination where she seeks both release and solace from the oppressive forces in her life.The poem's lyrical quality draws the reader into Ophelia's turmoil. Its rhythmic flow and evocative language heighten the raw emotion, creating a sense of unrelenting sorrow and a desperate quest for solace.

Song of Silence

My life a canvas, painted with their dreams,
My soul, wrapped around their fingers, screams.
An instrument in my father's eye,
A pawn cosplayed as a spy.
A frail damsel tossed in the bay,
No voice, no choice, just currents I obey.

Questions a thousand, plague my soul,
I - a beloved bairn or just a gullible ingénue?
Treacherous lucid moments I can't face,
The grotesque frenzy, Oh! Solace.
Amid life's wretchedness, a note stands clear,
A personal vow, unwavering, sincere,

Blood on his hands, whispers in my heart,
The final verdict, this world I must depart.
Rosemary, fennel, my parting benediction,
The willows benevolence, vessel to my freedom.
Water in my lungs, the suffocating pleasure,
Final moments, I call my own life's greatest treasure.

Lady MacBeth from MacBeth

Ballad

This poem is a ballad, a narrative form of poetry with origins in the oral traditions of medieval Europe. Traditionally passed down through generations, ballads were often sung or recited to a simple, rhythmic tune. Typically structured in short stanzas with a consistent rhyme scheme, a ballad tells a story, often about love, loss, or betrayal. The form's musical cadence and repetition allow the speaker's feelings and the unfolding events to resonate deeply, while the simple structure gives the poem a haunting, timeless quality.

Overview

This ballad gives voice to Lady Macbeth and captures her descent into guilt and despair through a rhythmic, lyrical narrative that blends love, ambition and remorse. Its structured cadence contrasts with her unraveling psyche, offering a poignant medium to convey her love, guilt, and ultimate resignation. The structured rhyme and rhythm reflects the tragic inevitability of her fate, while the emotive language reveals her internal conflict and unspoken tenderness for Macbeth.

Whispers of the Crown

A foul limped caitiff, they call me?
A fiend, a wretched heart of ice.
But doth not see a woman, by ambition tossed aside.
A wicked queen and a horrid sculpture of vice.

Despite the malevolent verity of my life,
My love for Macbeth rises high,
Cuts through the love of just a wife.
Musing about mine love's well being in the late nights of July.

The Sorceresses whisper twisted prophecies,
A twisted path, a throne for him and me.
But guilt and plans, morph into regrets,
And sleep, a traitor, steals my sanity away.

Rueing through the nights,
Overwhelming thoughts of bloody daggers and rough lines,
Sorry my love, but I doth die, for I have sinned,
In slumber's grip, my soul doth wander free,
As I ascend to the eternal garden by my own hand slain,
I leave you be, for I'm aware that you'll make it better, without me...

Hero from Much Ado ABout Nothing

Haiku

This poem is a haiku, a traditional form of Japanese poetry known for its simplicity and focus on nature or emotion. A haiku consists of three lines with a syllabic structure of 5-7-5, creating a concise and evocative snapshot. The form emphasizes brevity, vivid imagery, and a moment of insight or reflection, often leaving space for the reader's interpretation.

This poem is a creative twist on the traditional haiku form, I felt that Hero's depth of love, betrayal, and quiet suffering required more space. By combining three haikus, I've woven a layered narrative that honors the form's brevity while expanding its emotional and thematic reach.

Overview

The haiku form is ideal for Hero to express her emotions, as its brevity mirrors her fleeting, unspoken inner turmoil. This poem captures her love, betrayal, and quiet suffering through sharp, poignant moments, allowing her to convey deep emotions with clarity and restraint. The concise structure reflects her fading sense of self and hidden heartbreak, making her untold feelings resonate with a subtle yet powerful intensity.

Veil of Deceit

Don John's envy burns,
I fade, feigned death for honour
Truth brings love renewed.

Suitors come and go,
Claudio's sweet vows take root
Love blooms in secret.

Whispers weave a lie,
Honor slips through jealous hands
My heart breaks in shame.

Rosalind from As You Like It

Sonnet

This poem is a sonnet, a highly structured form of poetry known for its elegance and thematic depth. A sonnet consists of 14 lines, traditionally written in iambic pentameter, with a specific rhyme scheme depending on the type (e.g., Shakespearean or Petrarchan). The form's structure allows for a progression of ideas, often presenting a conflict or question in the first part and resolving it in the final lines, creating a sense of unity and closure.

Overview

This sonnet uses its structured rhyme and meter to mirror the tension between Rosalind's outward persona and her inner turmoil. The form allows her to express complex emotions—grief, longing, and acceptance—while subtly revealing her hidden identity and love. The progression from sorrow to solace reflects her journey of self-discovery, highlighting the freedom she finds in love and authenticity, beyond the constraints of societal expectations.

Love in Arden

By uncle's ire, exiled from courtly world,
To woods of Ardent where solace I seek,
Celia's amity, mine spirit enthralled,
Yet Mine's desolate heart is drowning and bleak.

With absence of his, a gnawing sorrow,
Desperate plea submerged, long lonely nights,
Yet fair fortune smiled, my heart forthwith followed,
In forest depths, where shadows veiled the light.

Behind stunning facade lies a brill mind.
Shielded by mine identity I hide,
Doth not take much to love, love truly blind.

Thus love endures, though outward form be changed,
And hearts entwined, where souls are interchanged.
In Arden's grove, true self and love unchained.

Portia** from **Merchant of Venice

Soliloquy

This poem is a soliloquy, a dramatic form of poetry in which a character expresses their inner thoughts and emotions aloud, typically when alone or unaware of being overheard. The soliloquy originates from classical Greek theater, where characters deliver monologues to reveal their inner thoughts. Soliloquies allow for deep introspection, providing insight into the speaker's mind, often revealing conflicting emotions, desires, or moral dilemmas.

Overview

The soliloquy becomes the ideal form for Portia to express her emotions, as it provides an intimate and unfiltered glimpse into her inner turmoil, free from the judgment and constraints of the world around her. Through this solitary reflection, she reveals her deepest vulnerabilities,the reflective tone reveals the tension between her loyalty to her father's will and her longing for freedom and passion, capturing the timeless conflict between societal expectations and the pursuit of individual passion and fulfillment.

The Casket of Fate

English barons, Scottish lords, German dukes,
Fair and noble beauty, they all vie for,
Yet, mine heart doth yearn for mine one true love,
Mayhap, fate shall soon bring us together.

The burning tears drop from my dismal eyes
The sweet royal blood trails down just like vines
Why must I live in neglect and sorrow?
For fulfilling my dead fathers morals.

Respect and admire I contain for him,
Wishes, I tend to complete without grim,
Yet, I find myself frantically praying,
That my farthingale is unveiled by him...

Bassanio's gaze, a dare and a plea,
My profuse heart, will I ever be free?
Tied by my sire's will, I am a vessel,
Tearing us both apart like a devil.

I shall wail or decease until I find,
Mine one true love, within my gaze and mind.
I shall turneth a deaf ear athwart all,
Biding for my beloved's ardent call.

With caskets three, my fate I dare to trust,
Will true love win or succumb into dust?

Katherina *from* ***The Taming of the Shrew***

Sestina

This poem is a sestina, a highly structured form of poetry characterized by its intricate pattern of word repetition. A sestina consists of six stanzas, each with six lines, followed by a three-line envoi (a concluding stanza). The defining feature is the rotation of six specific end words through each stanza in a fixed order, creating a weaving effect.

Overview

This sestina delves into Katherina's internal conflict as she navigates Petruchio's attempts to "tame" her, using the poem's repetitive structure to emphasize the cyclical nature of societal expectations imposed upon her. The rotating end-words—"tame," "unseen," "wild," "defiance," "demeanour," and "wed"—mirror her struggles with identity, autonomy, and the roles forced upon her as a woman. Through this intricate form, the poem captures her suppressed emotions, revealing the layers of resilience and rebellion beneath her seemingly subdued exterior.

Veiled and Unyielding

Petruchio schemes, his goal to tame me,
To mold me into the woman he wants, unseen.
They think they know me—Katherina, hard and wild—
They call me "shrew" and laugh at my defiance.
None pause to ask what drives this fierce demeanour,
They only see the tale of one unfit to wed.

Since childhood I knew what they all sought in a wife, wed
To service, sweet silence, and a docile hand. He'd tame me,
They said, break my spirit and strip away this demeanour,
For a woman's proper place is one unseen.
But I'll not bow to men's expectations, nor their scornful defiance,
For I am Katherina, not some dutiful lamb, nor mild.

They compare me to Bianca, my sister, tender and mild—
Men swarm to her, all eager to court and wed.
They call her "angel," the perfect bride without defiance,
But I, too bold, am left to his grip, where he will tame me.
I am blamed, dismissed, while she is ideal and unseen,
An easy prize, for those who crave a wife with meek demeanour.

Petruchio begins his "taming" with a twisted demeanour,
A mind bent on control, a heart far from mild.
Isolation and hunger are his tools, unseen,
To weaken my resolve until I am fit to wed,
Breaking my spirit, layer by layer, he will tame me,
Testing my patience with relentless taunts, squashing my defiance.

"A wife should serve," they say, their voices tinged with scorn and defiance.
She must smile, speak soft, with a courteous demeanour,
Speak only when bidden, obedient to please and tame me,
A vision of sweetness—never brash, never wild.
She exists to please and obey, nothing more, her mind bound to wed,
Sacrificing herself for her lord, her dreams unseen.

At last, my fiery words and stinging wit are unseen,
Lost in the mold he has carved with patience and defiance.
Some parts of me are changing, softening, and ready to wed,
Others remain, masked behind this "new" demeanour.
In silence I fume, my spirit tempered, wild
Yet subdued; he smiles to know he has tamed me.

In quiet I stand, unseen, a woman tamed yet wild,
Knowing defiance is but one side of a mannered demeanour.
To be wed is to play a role; he tamed me for all to see.

Titania from Midsummer's Night Dream

Free Verse

This poem is written in free verse, a form of poetry that lacks a fixed rhyme scheme or meter, allowing for greater flexibility and freedom of expression. Free verse enables the poet to craft a more natural flow of language, reflecting the speaker's emotions and thoughts without the constraints of traditional forms. This open structure allows the poem to explore complex themes and ideas with fluidity and individuality, emphasizing the power of language itself.

Overview

Free verse is the ideal form for Titania's expression as it mirrors the chaotic and unpredictable nature of her untold emotions, blending humor and frustration.. The poem mirrors Titania's regal voice, capturing her indignation, wit, and eventual triumph. The unstructured style aligns with her turbulent feelings and explores her journey as she reflects on Oberon's meddling and the ridiculousness of her plight. Yet, through her wit and resilience, Titania rises above the folly, teaching Oberon—and the reader—a lesson about respect and the folly of tampering with a queen's will.

Beneath the Moonlit Veil

Oberon, Oberon, Oberon,
Thy impish mien, thy witty prattle,
Thy grievous thirst for triumph vile,
Hath turned my love life to a jester's guile!

First, the ceaseless bick'ring strife,
Then Puck, with his potions most misbegot!
Thou hast betrayed me, Titania the Queen,
And cast me into a snare most obscene!

His woolly visage,
His floppy ears,
I sit bemused by his bewitched guise,
Whilst fairies titter with merry jeers, much to mine ire and sighs.

Oberon's countenance, bedecked with a smirk,
They jest at me? As I dote on Bottom.
Love encircles us, and a crown wrought of weeds,
This cursed potion yields the foulest of deeds!

Yet hark, dost thou suffer thy own device?
Oberon doth sigh, his heart enticed,
By jealous pangs greater than love's enchantment,
Thus my true love restored, free of asinine lament.

A lesson well taught, I hope 'tis so,
That Oberon and Puck might wiser grow.
Should fairies dare to sway a queen's desire,
Let it not be to an ass, 'neath the moonlit spire!

Acknowledgments

I would like to express my heartfelt gratitude to my parents for their unwavering support throughout the creation of this collection. Their encouragement, patience, and belief in my abilities have been a constant source of motivation. Thank you for always fostering my passion for writing and helping me bring this project to life. Your guidance and love have made this journey possible, and I am deeply grateful for everything you have done to support me along the way.

A special thank you to my teachers and mentors for their invaluable guidance, encouragement, and inspiration throughout this creative journey.

www.ingramcontent.com/pod-product-compliance
Lightning Source LLC
LaVergne TN
LVHW091244150826
845673LV00003B/1291

* 9 7 9 8 8 9 6 7 3 5 4 3 4 *